It's My Body

My Head

Lola M. Schaefer

Heinemann Library

Chicago, Illinois

© 2003 Heinemann Library
a division of Reed Elsevier Inc.
Chicago, IL

Customer Service 888-454-2279
Visit our website at www.heinemannlibrary.com

Designed by Sue Emerson, Heinemann Library; Page layout by Que-Net Media
Printed and bound in the United States by Lake Book Manufacturing, Inc.
Photo research by Jennifer Gillis

07 06 05 04 03
10 9 8 7 6 5 4 3 2 1

Library of Congress Cataloging-in-Publication Data
Schaefer, Lola M., 1950-
    My head / Lola M. Schaefer.
        v. cm. – (It's my body)
Includes index.

Contents: What is your head? – Where is your head? – What does your head look like? – What's inside your head? – What can you do with your head? – What is your face? – What do faces look like? – What is inside your face? – What can you do with your face? – Quiz – Picture glossary.
    ISBN 1-4034-0891-2 (HC), 1-4034-3483-2 (Pbk.)
    1. Head–Juvenile literature. [1. Head. 2. Face. 3. Human anatomy.]
I. Title. II. Series.
    QM535 .S355 2003
    612'.91–dc21

                              2002014740

Acknowledgments
The author and publishers are grateful to the following for permission to reproduce copyright material:
p. 4 Richard Hutchings/PhotoEdit; p. 5 Annie Griffiths Belt/Corbis; pp. 6, 8, 9, 14, 16, 18, 19, 20, 21, 22, 24 Brian Warling/Heinemann Library; p. 7 Robert Lifson/Heinemann Library; p. 10 BSIP/PhotoTake; p. 12 George Disario/Corbis; p. 13 LWA-Dann Tardif/Corbis; p. 15 Lindsay Hebberd/Corbis; p. 17L Sue Klemens/Stock Boston, Inc./PictureQuest; p. 17R Ann Purcell; Carl Purcell/Words & Pictures/PictureQuest; p. 23 row 1 (L-R) Custom Medical Stock Photo, Brian Warling/Heinemann Library; row 2 Custom Medical Stock Photo; row 3 Brian Warling/Heinemann Library; back cover (L-R) BSIP/PhotoTake, Brian Warling/Heinemann Library

Cover photograph by Brian Warling/Heinemann Library

Every effort has been made to contact copyright holders of any material reproduced in this book. Any omissions will be rectified in subsequent printings if notice is given to the publisher.

Special thanks to our advisory panel for their help in the preparation of this book:

Alice Bethke, Library Consultant
Palo Alto, CA

Eileen Day, Preschool Teacher
Chicago, IL

Kathleen Gilbert,
Second Grade Teacher
Round Rock, TX

Sandra Gilbert,
Library Media Specialist
Fiest Elementary School
Houston, TX

Jan Gobeille,
Kindergarten Teacher
Garfield Elementary
Oakland, CA

Angela Leeper,
Educational Consultant
North Carolina Department
of Public Instruction
Wake Forest, NC

Some words are shown in bold, **like this.**
You can find them in the picture glossary on page 23.

Contents

What Is Your Head?

Your head is part of your body.

Your body is made up of
many parts.

Each part of your body does a job.

Your head helps you talk, smell, see, and hear.

Where Is Your Head?

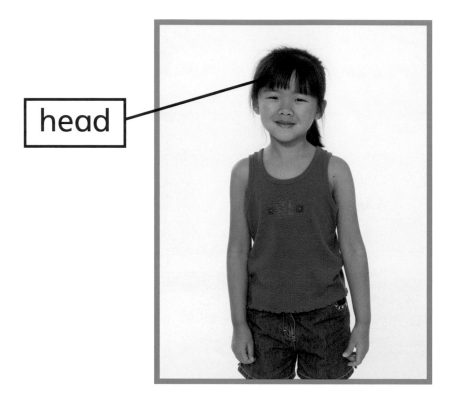

head

Your head is on top of your body.

Your neck joins your head to your body.

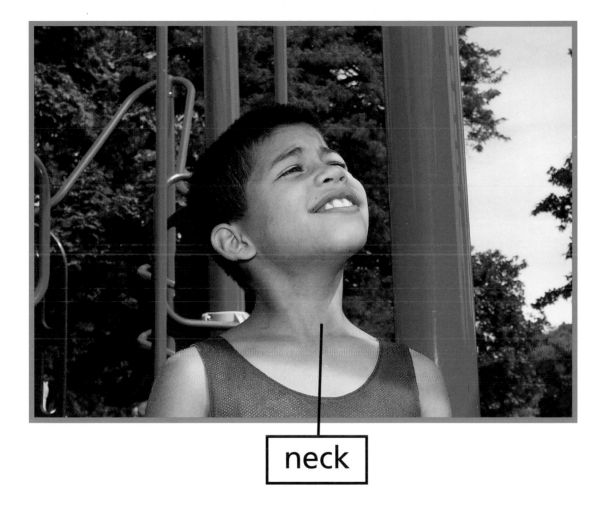

neck

Your neck has **joints** that help your head move.

Your head can move up, down, and around.

What Does Your Head Look Like?

Heads look like round balls.

Hair covers the top of most heads.

Grown-ups have bigger heads.

Children have smaller heads.

What Is Inside Your Head?

skull

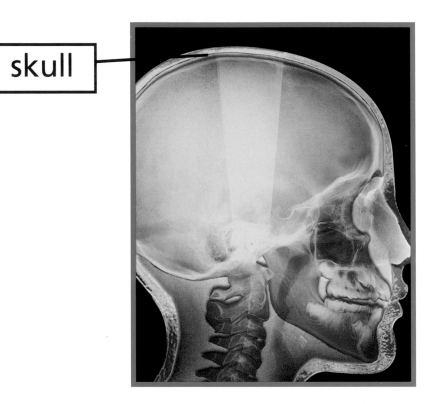

Muscles and **bones** are inside your head.

Your **skull** gives your head its shape.

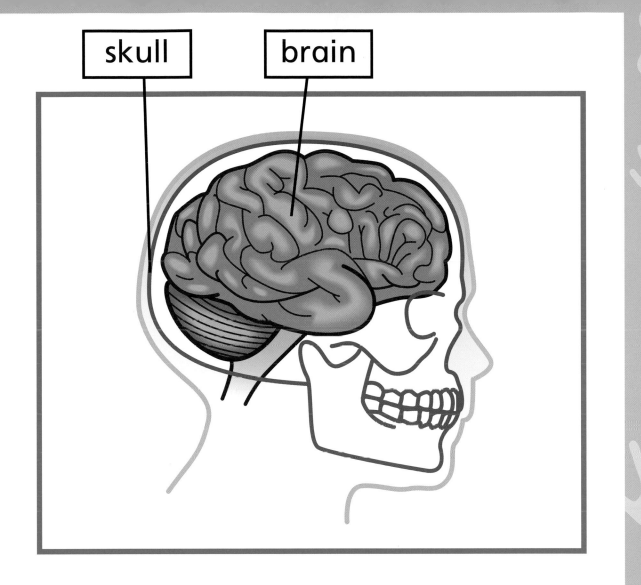

Your **brain** is inside your head.

Your skull keeps your brain safe.

What Can You Do with Your Head?

Your **brain** helps you think.

Your eyes help you see.

Your ears help you hear.

Your nose helps you breathe
and smell.

What Is Your Face?

hairline

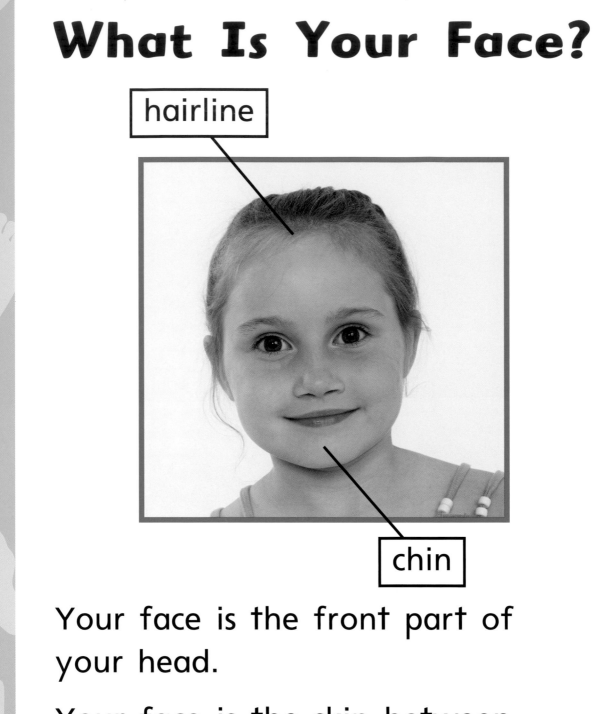

chin

Your face is the front part of your head.

Your face is the skin between your **hairline** and **chin**.

14

Your face has a mouth and nose.

It has two eyes and two ears.

What Do Faces Look Like?

Faces can be full and round.

They can be long and thin.

Some faces have smooth skin.

Other faces have many wrinkles.

What Is Inside Your Face?

Bones and **muscles** are inside your face.

Muscles help you show feelings.

A mouth is inside your face.

Your teeth and tongue are inside your mouth.

What Can You Do with Your Face?

Your face helps you show how you feel.

You can frown or cry.

You can make a funny sound.

You can smile and laugh.

Quiz

Can you guess what these are?

Look for the answers on page 24.

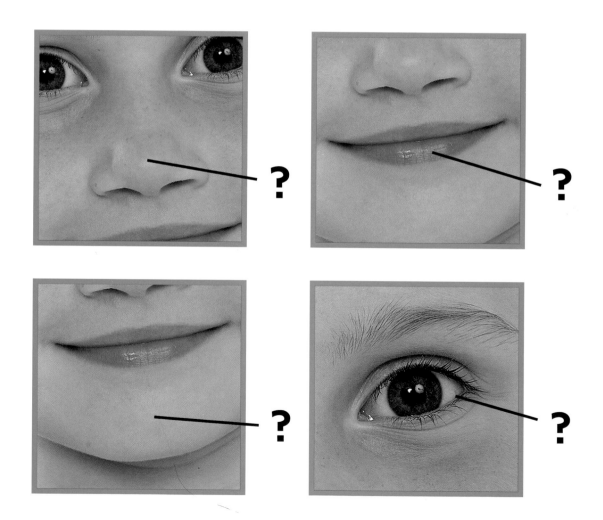

? ? ? ?

22

Picture Glossary

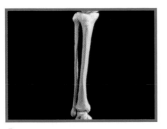

bone
pages 10, 18

hairline
page 14

muscle
pages 10, 18

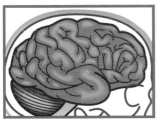

brain
pages 11, 12

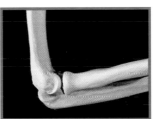

joint
page 7

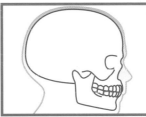

skull
pages 10, 11

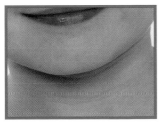

chin
page 14

Note to Parents and Teachers

Reading for information is an important part of a child's literacy development. Learning begins with a question about something. Help children think of themselves as investigators and researchers by encouraging their questions about the world around them. Each chapter in this book begins with a question. Read the question together. Look at the pictures. Talk about what you think the answer might be. Then read the text to find out if your predictions were correct. Think of other questions you could ask about the topic, and discuss where you might find the answers. Assist children in using the picture glossary and the index to practice new vocabulary and research skills.

Index

Answers to quiz on page 22

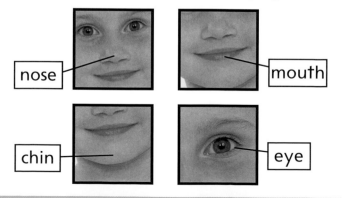

24